# DOWNSIZING
## The Family Home
### A WORKBOOK

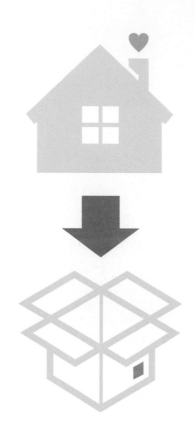

# DOWNSIZING
## The Family Home
### A WORKBOOK
#### WHAT TO SAVE | WHAT TO LET GO

## Marni Jameson
*Nationally syndicated home and lifestyle columnist*

STERLING
New York

Real Possibilities

## DEDICATED TO PIPPIN — M. J.

STERLING
New York

An Imprint of Sterling Publishing Co., Inc.
1166 Avenue of the Americas
New York, NY 10036

ISBN 978-1-4549-2652-8

Distributed in Canada by Sterling Publishing Co., Inc.
c/o Canadian Manda Group, 664 Annette Street
Toronto, Ontario M6S 2C8, Canada
Distributed in the United Kingdom by GMC Distribution Services
Castle Place, 166 High Street, Lewes, East Sussex BN7 1XU, England
Distributed in Australia by NewSouth Books
45 Beach Street, Coogee NSW 2034, Australia

For information about custom editions, special sales, and premium and corporate purchases,
please contact Sterling Special Sales at 800-805-5489 or specialsales@sterlingpublishing.com.

Manufactured in China

2 4 6 8 10 9 7 5 3

sterlingpublishing.com

## "*Make us heirs of all eternity.*"

—WILLIAM SHAKESPEARE

# Contents

# Introduction

## *Why This Journal?*
## *Because Memories (Not Stuff) Matter*

*But it's my life!* Dire as that sounds, that is exactly the sentiment we feel when facing the challenge of purging possessions collected and clung to through the years. Yes, we know it's just stuff, but it's our stuff, or a loved one's stuff, and it represents a life.

We tell ourselves, "I matter. My loved ones matter. Life matters."

Somehow, we transfer all that mattering onto things. Which is why getting rid of old belongings makes us feel as if we are erasing history. Keeping them is a way of telling the world: My life counts! Or so we think.

This emotion becomes amplified when we are dealing with the belongings of a loved one who has passed on, or who is moving into smaller quarters or assisted living. By clinging to their things, we cling to them. Besides, clearing out their worldly possessions feels disrespectful. If they have died, we half expect them to reach down from the heavens and smack us.

The guilt is real.

Letting go of all the dishes, linens, books, tools, artwork, clothing, letters, photos, and furniture—things that once mattered (or why would we still have them?)—feels like sweeping an eraser across the chalkboard. All that's left is the dust.

But let go, we must.

Though we know intellectually that people aren't their things, and that clinging to old stuff will never bring back the past, or loved ones we've lost, most people ardently avoid a task that all of us must eventually face—the job of clearing out a houseful of memories.

The alternative, however—keeping everything forever—is burdensome, impractical, and costly. Excess stuff consumes time, energy, money, and space. It becomes literally dead weight, a heavy load that keeps us from enjoying the present and relishing the future. Imagine the extreme: Everyone saves everything and hands it all down to the next generation, who also saves everything, creating one giant snowball of old stuff, filling our living spaces, attics, garages, and storage units to capacity.

We need a plan.

The inspiration for this interactive journal, or workbook, came shortly after my book *Downsizing the Family Home* was released. An editor at the publishing house who wasn't involved with the project picked up the book because she was about to clear out her parents' home.

"I loved this book," she later told me. "I leaned on it to help me through one of the toughest times of my life. I only wish it had come with a journal."

"A journal?"

"You know, a workbook to help sort all the emotions along with the stuff."

I later learned she wasn't the only one who felt that way. In fact, what had kept me going as I cleared out my dear parents' home was writing about it in my weekly column and calling on experts for support. That and recording it all in *Downsizing the Family Home* was all that stood between me and losing my sanity. What this editor and what other readers craved was a place to tell their story, a book in which to chronicle what they were going through, how it felt, what they did with all the stuff; in short, a repository where they could preserve the memories—not the stuff—and thus preserve both their sanity and the sanctity of their homes.

In my last book, as well as in my weekly syndicated column, "At Home with Marni Jameson," which runs in newspapers across the country, I took you through my excruciating journey of clearing out my elderly parents' home of nearly fifty years, after they moved into assisted living. (They have both since died, after living into their nineties.) This workbook is a place for you to chronicle your downsizing journey. Whether paring down your own household so you don't burden the next generation—please!—or clearing out the home of a loved one, this workbook is designed to help you through.

This interactive journal will not only steer and support you as you go but also will help you work through blocks, preserve memories, and hold on to just enough stuff. You can also use it to create a record of what you sold where and for how much, and who in the family got the grandfather clock or the diamond brooch. This workbook will guide you personally, practically, and (almost) painlessly through the process.

From defining your downsizing goals and working through the resistance, to categorizing the tough stuff and deciding whether or where to sell or donate it, this journal is where you can respectfully pay homage to belongings as you let go and, finally, pay tribute to the people and homes you've loved.

The key to making this journal work for you is to make this about your journey. No two experiences are the same. Although the prompts are here to guide you as you dive in and delve through the rough, icy waters, don't feel compelled to reply to every one, or even to work through the pages chronologically. Respond to the questions that resonate. Come back later to fill in gaps, and layer in photos and scraps of fabric. As you work through the journal, in your own way and in your own time, your story will emerge.

And it will be worth keeping.

# PART ONE

# Nostalgia

I love the word *nostalgia*, which combines the Greek words for going home and pain. That is the combination we embrace as we downsize a home that has meant something to us. And home, by nature, always does. So to start this journey and to get mentally prepared, spend some time, in this opening section of your workbook, writing down what brought you to this point.

I

# Finding Your Purpose

Almost all of us will reach a point in life when we need to downsize. The reasons, like the stages of our lives, vary. Some downsizers—or better, *rightsizers*—want the financial freedom of living with less. Some are moving to a smaller home. Some are divorcing. Some are clearing out the home of an older parent, a spouse, or another loved one who has moved into assisted living or passed on. Some are lightening up so they don't leave a burden to the next generation. Sometimes it's a combination.

Whatever the reason, downsizing stirs feelings of loss, sadness, longing, and grief—all real and valid feelings. Nevertheless, like a tree dropping its leaves to make room for new growth, letting go is a healthy part of the cycle of life. By cleaning house, literally and metaphorically, you shed what's holding you back and make room for renewal.

Homes are not static. Like the lives within, they evolve and change. Kids come and go, in-laws move in and out, couples become single, singles become couples, seniors move into homes that offer more assistance. And along the way, households—ideally—expand and contract to accommodate these transitions. Our job, then, is to continually edit the contents of our homes so they support and reflect the life that's now, not the one that was.

Living in the past truly does rob us of the present and the future.

## BEGIN YOUR JOURNEY

The first step in your downsizing journey is to clarify why you're downsizing. Simply defining the reasons can be motivating and, when you're feeling overwhelmed—which you will—having these reasons in writing will help you stay the course. When you ask yourself why you are doing this, come back to these pages to find your purpose.

❯ What has brought me to this moment? (This story is the beginning of your journey.)

_____

_____

_____

_____

_____

_____

_____

_____

_____

_____

》 I know I must do this because . . .

_____

_____

_____

_____

_____

_____

_____

_____

_____

_____

_____

_____

_____

_____

_____

_____

❱ Why is this experience so bittersweet? Describe the bitter and the sweet. This is sad or bitter because . . .

_____

_____

_____

_____

_____

_____

_____

❱ This is good or sweet because . . .

_____

_____

_____

_____

_____

_____

_____

## 2

# Creating a Mind-Set

As we go through the downsizing journey, we know intellectually that we can't keep everything we want to keep, but our hearts cling. What we need to understand is that these conflicted feelings are not about the material objects. They are about the primitive emotions connected to the four Ls: loss, legacy, legend, and love. In short, sorting through a household makes us face our own mortality: the passage of time, life and death, where we've been, where we haven't been, where we are in our lives, successes, and regrets. But what will pull us through are our guiding lights. What are yours? Stay focused and move forward.

## START WITH THE END IN MIND

Visualize, for a moment, your goal. Imagine what the end of your downsizing process looks like. Is it a completely cleaned-out house, room in the garage to park both cars, extra space in the orderly closets? Do you see a well-appointed smaller home where you have all you need and no more?

❭ Describe the vision of your goal. Ask yourself, what does my light at the end of the tunnel look like?

_____

_____

_____

_____

_____

_____

❭ Downsizing has many upsides. List all the benefits of lightening up and letting go.

_____

_____

_____

_____

_____

_____

❯ If you are clearing out a loved one's home, ask yourself, what would he or she be telling me? For instance, I channeled my father, who, whenever I felt overwhelmed by a big project, used to say to me, "Keep your eye on the ball." What would your loved one say to motivate you?

_____

_____

_____

_____

_____

_____

_____

_____

_____

_____

_____

_____

❯ By letting go, I am honoring my loved one's memory because . . .

_____

_____

_____

_____

_____

_____

_____

_____

_____

_____

_____

_____

_____

_____

_____

_____

## FINDING YOUR MANTRA

I used the mantra "Need, Use, Love" as the filter for deciding what to keep, toss, donate, or sell from the voluminous contents of my childhood home, and also from my own home, as I moved on and made changes in my personal life. In other words, to see if a belonging would make the "keep" pile, I asked: Do I need it? Will I use it? Do I love it? The item needed to pass at least one of those filters—and, even better, all three.

INSIDE TIP: *When sorting through possessions, apply the "Need, Use, Love" test. If you don't need an item, it's not something you regularly use, or you can't honestly say you love it, then don't keep it.*

If you don't love an item, why keep it in your life? Or, if you already have something like the object you're wavering over, and the other version is better, why have a duplicate? If the item has served its useful life for you (say a highchair or a crib), or you haven't needed or used it in ten years, and it is still in good condition, let it serve someone else.

"Need, Use, Love" works for me, but you may work to shape your own litmus test. Ultimately, your filter should be something that is personal to you.

As you shape your own mantra for what to keep and what to let go of, beware of thoughts that trap you into clinging too much: *It's still in good condition. I don't need it now, but I might someday. It was expensive. So-and-so gave it to me.* Spend some time coming up with your own mantra, or filter, whether it's "Need, Use, Love" or something personal to you. Record your mantra on the next page.

❯ Here is my mantra for what I will keep:

_____

_____

_____

_____

_____

_____

_____

_____

_____

_____

_____

_____

_____

❯ If "Need, Use, Love" is your mantra, define what each of those terms means to you and give an example. For instance, I have my grandmother's wooden rolling pin. It is my only rolling pin, so I need it. I love how it feels in my hand and its functional but plain design. I use it when I bake, just as she did, which makes me feel connected to her.

*Need*

_____

_____

_____

_____

*Use*

_____

_____

_____

_____

*Love*

_____

_____

_____

_____

❯ These are the common refrains that make me cling to possessions, thoughts I must learn to ignore or override. I can choose not to be tempted.

_____

_____

_____

_____

_____

_____

_____

_____

_____

_____

_____

_____

_____

_____

》 When one of those old refrains plays, here's how I will respond:

_____

_____

_____

_____

_____

_____

_____

_____

_____

_____

_____

_____

_____

_____

## TRIGGER POINTS

Homes are loaded—literally and figuratively. By nature, homes are filled not only with memories, but also with belongings, including heirlooms that carry tremendous sentimental and sometimes monetary value. As a result, taking apart the family home triggers many mixed feelings, all at once. The process is emotionally, mentally, and physically overwhelming. Knowing that going in provides a huge leg up.

For instance, in my parents' home, the dining room table where we had all our family dinners was especially hard for me to part with. I made all kinds of rationalizations for why I needed to keep it, although I had a lovely dining room table already, and surely didn't want to ship this one across the country to my house. Yet I turned down the only offer I had from a buyer who wanted the table, because I couldn't let go. Eventually, I gave the table and its chairs to a former neighbor, a young woman I used to babysit who was now a single mom. That felt right.

Years ago, I got attached to a rocking chair I got as a gift when I was pregnant with my first baby. This is the chair in which I rocked her, and later her sister, for hours. The chair was special to me and held many memories. But when I moved from my house as an adult needing to rightsize and reshape my life, I had no place for it in my new home. While it was hard to let go of, I donated the chair to a women's shelter, where I knew it would continue to comfort others.

Besides special pieces of furniture, so many things in a home can trip us up, such as: family photos, military memorabilia, artwork, letters, books, an old grandfather clock. These belongings can trigger emotional—and often irrational—urges to cling. Think about your own trigger points, and record them on the next page.

❭ List areas or objects in your home, or in your loved one's home, that are loaded trigger points.

_____

_____

_____

_____

_____

_____

_____

_____

_____

_____

_____

_____

_____

_____

_____

*"Where we love is home—home that our feet may leave, but not our hearts."*

—OLIVER WENDELL HOLMES SR.

## SURVIVING THE SENTIMENTAL

As you go through this process, no matter how clearheaded you are when you start, you will likely get waylaid and fall into sinkholes of sentiment. That's normal. When that happens, having thoughts—those "guiding lights"—at the ready can feel like a helping hand pulling you out of the quicksand. But these guiding lights only work if you keep them turned on.

Here are a couple I used: "Just because something is still useful doesn't make it useful to me." Also this: "My parents wouldn't want their household of things to burden me."

INSIDE TIP: *As you sort through your own home or a parent's, your biggest worry will likely be: What if I get rid of something and regret it? Guess what? You will. But don't let that stop you from purging. Accept that the process is not perfect, and that you will make mistakes. Fortunately, you will make many, many more good decisions, which will far outweigh the few poor ones.*

When I feel overwhelmed, these thoughts—or guiding lights—will keep me going:

_____

_____

_____

_____

_____

❯ Knowing others will use and benefit from my cherished furnishings helps replace feelings of loss with feelings of gratefulness that I can help others. Here are some of the people or places that I would like to make better with my gift:

_____

_____

_____

_____

_____

_____

_____

_____

_____

_____

_____

_____

# PART TWO

# Endowment

"The endowment effect" is a term psychologists use to describe our need to cling to possessions, especially those that belonged to a loved one. Any belonging that someone you love bought, made, or used a lot will never be neutral. It carries an emotional charge, because we transfer feelings onto it in the same way a child transfers feelings of comfort and security onto a blanket or a stuffed bear. Think of all the significance we put into a wedding ring. Each one of our belongings has a story, and that story connects us to a place or a time or a person, or all three. We remember where we bought it, whom we were with, the places we wore it. The stories, not the items, are what make letting go so difficult.

**3**

# Understanding Attachment

When we are going through a loved one's belongings, we often struggle to let go because the items become merged with the person. Letting go further reminds us that everything in life is temporary.

We worry that if we let go of a loved one's stuff, we will lose them. But that's not true. Their story will continue with or without their physical possessions. Understanding the phenomenon of the endowment effect—that the mere owning of something increases our perception of its value—can help us detach. We can start to separate our loved one from their belongings.

In her book *The Year of Magical Thinking*, Joan Didion writes of the grief she experienced after her husband died suddenly. In one of the book's most moving passages—and there are many—she talks about going through his closet and not being able to give away his shoes, because "he will need them when he comes back."

Mostly we cling to things for irrational reasons. The more clearly we can see that truth, the easier it is to let go. Whether you keep an item or let it go doesn't change your attachment to the person. The person, like your own past, lives in your heart and mind.

## FACE YOUR FEARS

Even though we can see the many benefits of clearing out a home, relinquishing belongings—whether ours or a loved one's—stirs up feelings of anxiety, pain, sadness, and loss. On top of those feelings is the fear of forgetting. We worry that we will erase the past if we give up old belongings, or that we'll extinguish our loved one's memory. Or, as in Didion's case, that the deceased may come back and need them.

But the alternative—holding on—results in mounds of useless clutter that take away from our quality of life today.

In other words, the stuff of the past becomes a barrier to moving forward and to experiencing the joys of the present and the promises of the future.

We all have enough stuff. Letting go may feel as if we're obliterating the past, but the past will still be there. Take a few moments to dig deep and express what you're afraid of losing.

❭ Why is letting go so hard? What am I afraid of? What am I avoiding?

_____

_____

_____

_____

_____

_____

❯ Which belongings do I endow with sentimental value, and why?

_____

_____

_____

_____

_____

_____

_____

_____

_____

_____

_____

_____

_____

_____

_____

_____

❱ What about my loved one do I really want to hold on to?

_____

_____

_____

_____

_____

_____

❱ What qualities about that person do I want to remember?

_____

_____

_____

_____

_____

_____

_____

❯ When in the past have I let go of something that was hard to relinquish?
How did that feel? Was I ultimately relieved?

_____

_____

_____

_____

_____

_____

❯ Does knowing how that experience turned out help prepare me for what
I'm facing now?

_____

_____

_____

_____

_____

_____

_____

❯ In past moves or house clearings, what box, closet, or cupboard
was I most afraid to open and sort through? A grown child's toy box?
A collection of college memorabilia? Why?

_____

_____

_____

_____

_____

_____

❯ What memories surfaced? Does knowing how I came through that help
me now?

_____

_____

_____

_____

_____

_____

❯ How do I hope my loved ones remember me? What physical legacy do I want to leave behind and why?

_____

_____

_____

_____

_____

_____

❯ Which of my possessions do I hope stay in the family? Which ones would I like donated to a cause I care about?

_____

_____

_____

_____

_____

_____

*"Take only memories,
leave nothing but footprints."*

—CHIEF SEATTLE

# 4

# Finding Freedom

So often the scariest moves in life involve a leap of faith. Whether the change involves getting married, going off to college, having a baby, accepting a new job, or moving, selling, or buying a house, you simply don't know what lies on the other side until you get there. Trading the known for the unknown takes courage. The same is true of downsizing. We fear what we don't know. We fear what it will feel like not to have the things we have now. We fear that we will regret letting go of something we'll later wish we hadn't. We fear we will erase the past. We fear the irreparable.

What you don't yet know, however, is how good it will feel to be free of the burden—the avalanche—of the past. What a relief it will be to have room in your garage to park two cars, to have an empty attic, to have a property free and clear so you can sell it, to have streamlined closets and cupboards that have only what you need, use, and love—and no more. You don't yet know how right, reverent, and respectful it will feel to have only those carefully chosen few mementos that belonged to your loved ones, and that pay homage to their lives.

When you let go of the past, you discover the space to live life in the present, in anticipation of the next chapter.

❯ This is what the freedom that comes from cleaning or clearing out my family home will look and feel like.

_____

_____

_____

_____

_____

_____

❯ Here is how letting go and lightening up will help me to live better now and for the rest of my life.

_____

_____

_____

_____

_____

_____

_____

## Memo to Parents: The Kids Don't Want Your Stuff

Parents of grown children, please sit down with a sobering cup of black coffee. I have some harsh news for you: Your kids don't want your stuff. It's not that they don't love you. They don't love your furniture. All those family treasures—the china hutch, the collectible figurines, the antique maps, your thimble collection, the heirloom sideboard—may be precious to you, but to your kids, not so much.

Many of you will argue that you are being generous, and that your kids don't appreciate the quality of the items you paid dearly for; that you cannot bear to part with these testaments to the family tree and thus they shouldn't either. One day, they will surely regret the error of their ways, so you are going to hold out until that day comes, when they come around and thank you for not listening to them, because you knew best all along.

My friends, that is pure fantasy. Whenever I speak on this topic, I get two responses: groans of those recognizing themselves—I know, it burns—and applause from the adult children, who really, really don't want the carved headboard, or the grandfather clock.

A walk through any antique or consignment store will testify to this. These stores are brimming with brown wood furniture, figurines, dishes, and borderline artwork that parents could not foist onto their kids.

At the risk of becoming unpopular, let me try to save you generations of strife by offering the following advice:

- *Ask your kids what they want, and believe them*. Telling yourself the kids want your stuff—even when they say they don't—is either a form of denial or laziness or both. Some will take furnishings they like if they can see it working for them. Get rid of the rest.

- *Your kids want to create their own lives*. They also want their own style, not yours. Plus, many already have stuff. If your furniture is still useful, sell or donate it to someone who does want it.

- *Don't lay on a guilt trip*. Please do not say things like, "When I'm gone, I want you to have my twelve-foot mahogany dining-room table and eight chairs, because that would mean a lot to me." They don't need your furniture to hold you in their hearts. Give them the gift of freedom.

❯ How will my letting go and lightening up now benefit the next generation?

_____

_____

_____

_____

_____

_____

_____

❯ If I don't let go and lighten up, what kind of a burden am I creating for the next generation? How can my behavior now serve as an example?

_____

_____

_____

_____

_____

_____

_____

# PART THREE

# Downsizing

Getting mentally prepared to purge a household is half the battle. After that, you have to get physical. The most successful downsizing efforts begin by making a rough cut, and separating all belongings into four main groups: toss, sell or donate, keep, and don't know. If you're in the home, you might try grouping these items in separate rooms: garbage in the garage, items for sale or donation in the living room. Whatever approach you take, momentum is crucial. Remember your guiding lights, dive in, and persevere. The hardest part is starting. Procrastination only makes the process harder.

5

# Divide and Conquer

R eady to roll up your sleeves? This is going to get messy. Whether liquidating or radically downsizing a household, chances are you will want to have an estate, garage, or yard sale. (See the difference between these types of sales in Chapter 8.) Now, you need to make your rough cuts: keep, toss, or sell. (With a few exceptions, what you don't sell, you will donate. We'll discuss donations in Chapter 10.)

The first step is to go room by room, with a systematic, divide-and-conquer strategy, so you don't get overwhelmed. Empty all drawers, cupboards, and closets, and then plow through the contents. As you sort, think of the process as separating wheat from chaff—or keep, toss, and sell. Have a lot of large, heavy-duty trash bags at hand, and move all trash to one location, such as the curb or garage, outside the main house. (You may need to rent a haul-away trash container.) Organize the "wheat"—the items to sell—so that like items are together. For instance, put all lamps together, and group all artwork, jewelry, kitchenware, and so forth. Bundling items now will make preparing for sale day easier.

 INSIDE TIP: *Packets of colored-dot stickers can be used for sorting and, eventually, for pricing items for sale.*

I used colored dot stickers to organize and sort. You can devise your own system, but I put red stickers on items I wanted to keep, green stickers on items to sell, blue on items to donate, and yellow on items I was unsure about. When you hit an item that makes you come to a halt, one that you just aren't sure what to do with, put it aside with a yellow "yield" sticker to address later. Items to be tossed don't get a sticker.

If you do this first step right and get serious about throwing items away, you should significantly reduce the bulk. This is the low-hanging fruit.

## SEPARATING TRASH FROM TREASURE

Although most of us know what trash is, let me help you. First, remove your rose-colored glasses and give items an honest appraisal. Throw away anything open or partly used (cosmetics, hair products, condiments). Toss anything that is broken, stained, past its prime, rusted, missing parts, not working, or obsolete (such as cassette tape players). Get rid of most paper items, including all greeting cards. The exceptions are important documents, such as property titles, marriage and birth certificates, wills, current insurance policies, and any certificates of authenticity related to household art, antiques, or rugs. These should go into a separate pile for scanning.

》 When I separated the wheat from the chaff, here's what went into the chaff pile:

_____

_____

_____

_____

_____

_____

_____

_____

_____

_____

_____

_____

This process alone reduced my bulk by _____ percent. Progress!

## ORGANIZING TO SELL

Now, you should have left only items that have possible market value, serious sentimental value to you, or both. The next task is to get the items you'd like to sell ready for sale. If you were bundling as you purged, organizing by category should be simple. You want a lot of flat surfaces. Borrow some folding tables, and use existing counters. Now categorize. Put all books in one place, all figurines in another. Do the same for table and bed linens, silk floral arrangements, baskets, purses, etc.

If you are having an estate sale inside the house, put items in the appropriate living areas as much as possible. For instance: books in the den, kitchen utensils in the kitchen, and all gardening supplies outside on the patio table. Pull together all household cleaning items in one batch and put them in the utility room. Once all your sale items are grouped, you are ready to price.

If you come across items you want to donate instead of sell, such as clothing, you can start a separate donation pile now. (The trunk of a car or back of a pickup is a good place.) Later, you can add to it any sale items that don't sell.

❭ As I sifted and sorted, I ended up with these broad categories of goods to sell. Below, list your categories and any related comments—*I can't believe Mom had sixty-three vases!*

_____

_____

_____

_____

_____

_____

_____

_____

_____

_____

_____

_____

_____

"The secret of getting started is breaking your complex, overwhelming tasks into small manageable tasks, and then starting on the first one."

—MARK TWAIN

## PRICING: A GAME OF "HOW LOW CAN YOU GO?"

As you price, keep this overarching tenet in mind: If you want it to go, keep it low. When practical, give one price for a whole batch of goods, say, all the kitchen utensils or all the mops, brooms, and cleaning items. Do not try to price every individual item. Rather, offer vases for two dollars each. Do not price items for what you think they would sell for in a retail or consignment store. Price items based on what it would be worth to you to be rid of them. (For a more detailed discussion of pricing, see Chapter 7 of the companion book, *Downsizing the Family Home*.)

INSIDE TIP: *If you believe you or your loved one could have items of significant value, this is the time to have an appraiser come through the house. This might keep you from selling a painting worth $5,000 for $50. If nothing else, an appraiser could give you some peace of mind.*

When pricing my items, here's how I approached it, along with some examples of the sticker prices I put on things:

_____

_____

_____

_____

_____

_____

**Item**                                              **Sticker Price**

## BUT I CAN'T LET GO!

At this stage, you will probably be inclined to keep too much. Look at the red-stickered items that you are reluctant to sell, and think hard about why you feel so attached to them and whether you really have room for them in your life. I had trouble parting with the antique marble-topped table that was my nightstand as a girl, but shipping it cross-country would have been cost prohibitive, and I really didn't have a place for it. See my tips below for how to choose what to hold on to.

INSIDE TIP: *As you plow through and sort out, here are some filters you can use to decide what to keep.*

- *Forget value, and instead choose meaning.*
- *Choose small over large.*
- *Pick what makes your life better today.*
- *Keep something that comes with a story.*
- *Lose the guilt. How you love someone lives in your heart, not in an inanimate object.*

› List here the items you're afraid to let go of. Don't worry, listing them doesn't mean you have to let them go. Just take a closer look. And should you decide to part with them, don't despair. Later in this book, you will have a chance to memorialize these precious items.

_____

_____

_____

_____

❯ Take a look at the list again and write down why you don't want to let go. What do you think you might regret?

_____

_____

_____

_____

_____

_____

_____

_____

_____

_____

_____

_____

_____

But I am going to let go. I feel it's the right decision because . . .

❭ Remember, the line between bestow and burden is thin. You don't want to carry the burden of your parents' belongings, nor do you want to burden your children. With that in mind, answer this: What would my loved ones want me to hold on to of theirs?

_____

_____

_____

_____

_____

_____

_____

_____

_____

_____

_____

_____

_____

# 6
# Sorting It Out

s you move through the home, one room at a time, use the spaces here to help you sort. The list doesn't have to be exhaustive, but it should serve to give you an overview of what you're dealing with. Next to each item, check the box for Keep, Toss, Sell, or Unsure. (In Chapter 11, we'll tackle the "I don't know" items—your pile of postponement.) As you list and sort, apply the organizing tips discussed in the last chapter. Bundling and stickering items as you go can save you time when you're ready to sell or donate these belongings.

**Bedrooms**                                                     Keep    Toss    Sell    Unsure

| | Keep | Toss | Sell | Unsure |
|---|---|---|---|---|
| _____ | ☐ | ☐ | ☐ | ☐ |
| _____ | ☐ | ☐ | ☐ | ☐ |
| _____ | ☐ | ☐ | ☐ | ☐ |
| _____ | ☐ | ☐ | ☐ | ☐ |
| _____ | ☐ | ☐ | ☐ | ☐ |
| _____ | ☐ | ☐ | ☐ | ☐ |

## Bedrooms

|  | Keep | Toss | Sell | Unsure |
|---|---|---|---|---|
| _____ | ☐ | ☐ | ☐ | ☐ |
| _____ | ☐ | ☐ | ☐ | ☐ |
| _____ | ☐ | ☐ | ☐ | ☐ |
| _____ | ☐ | ☐ | ☐ | ☐ |
| _____ | ☐ | ☐ | ☐ | ☐ |
| _____ | ☐ | ☐ | ☐ | ☐ |
| _____ | ☐ | ☐ | ☐ | ☐ |
| _____ | ☐ | ☐ | ☐ | ☐ |
| _____ | ☐ | ☐ | ☐ | ☐ |
| _____ | ☐ | ☐ | ☐ | ☐ |
| _____ | ☐ | ☐ | ☐ | ☐ |
| _____ | ☐ | ☐ | ☐ | ☐ |
| _____ | ☐ | ☐ | ☐ | ☐ |
| _____ | ☐ | ☐ | ☐ | ☐ |
| _____ | ☐ | ☐ | ☐ | ☐ |
| _____ | ☐ | ☐ | ☐ | ☐ |
| _____ | ☐ | ☐ | ☐ | ☐ |
| _____ | ☐ | ☐ | ☐ | ☐ |

## Bedrooms

|  | Keep | Toss | Sell | Unsure |
|---|---|---|---|---|
| _____ | ☐ | ☐ | ☐ | ☐ |
| _____ | ☐ | ☐ | ☐ | ☐ |
| _____ | ☐ | ☐ | ☐ | ☐ |
| _____ | ☐ | ☐ | ☐ | ☐ |
| _____ | ☐ | ☐ | ☐ | ☐ |
| _____ | ☐ | ☐ | ☐ | ☐ |
| _____ | ☐ | ☐ | ☐ | ☐ |
| _____ | ☐ | ☐ | ☐ | ☐ |
| _____ | ☐ | ☐ | ☐ | ☐ |
| _____ | ☐ | ☐ | ☐ | ☐ |
| _____ | ☐ | ☐ | ☐ | ☐ |
| _____ | ☐ | ☐ | ☐ | ☐ |
| _____ | ☐ | ☐ | ☐ | ☐ |
| _____ | ☐ | ☐ | ☐ | ☐ |
| _____ | ☐ | ☐ | ☐ | ☐ |
| _____ | ☐ | ☐ | ☐ | ☐ |
| _____ | ☐ | ☐ | ☐ | ☐ |
| _____ | ☐ | ☐ | ☐ | ☐ |

## Kitchen

|  | Keep | Toss | Sell | Unsure |
|---|---|---|---|---|
| _____ | ☐ | ☐ | ☐ | ☐ |
| _____ | ☐ | ☐ | ☐ | ☐ |
| _____ | ☐ | ☐ | ☐ | ☐ |
| _____ | ☐ | ☐ | ☐ | ☐ |
| _____ | ☐ | ☐ | ☐ | ☐ |
| _____ | ☐ | ☐ | ☐ | ☐ |
| _____ | ☐ | ☐ | ☐ | ☐ |
| _____ | ☐ | ☐ | ☐ | ☐ |
| _____ | ☐ | ☐ | ☐ | ☐ |
| _____ | ☐ | ☐ | ☐ | ☐ |
| _____ | ☐ | ☐ | ☐ | ☐ |
| _____ | ☐ | ☐ | ☐ | ☐ |
| _____ | ☐ | ☐ | ☐ | ☐ |
| _____ | ☐ | ☐ | ☐ | ☐ |
| _____ | ☐ | ☐ | ☐ | ☐ |
| _____ | ☐ | ☐ | ☐ | ☐ |
| _____ | ☐ | ☐ | ☐ | ☐ |
| _____ | ☐ | ☐ | ☐ | ☐ |

## Kitchen

| | Keep | Toss | Sell | Unsure |
|---|---|---|---|---|
| _____ | ☐ | ☐ | ☐ | ☐ |
| _____ | ☐ | ☐ | ☐ | ☐ |
| _____ | ☐ | ☐ | ☐ | ☐ |
| _____ | ☐ | ☐ | ☐ | ☐ |
| _____ | ☐ | ☐ | ☐ | ☐ |
| _____ | ☐ | ☐ | ☐ | ☐ |
| _____ | ☐ | ☐ | ☐ | ☐ |
| _____ | ☐ | ☐ | ☐ | ☐ |
| _____ | ☐ | ☐ | ☐ | ☐ |
| _____ | ☐ | ☐ | ☐ | ☐ |
| _____ | ☐ | ☐ | ☐ | ☐ |
| _____ | ☐ | ☐ | ☐ | ☐ |
| _____ | ☐ | ☐ | ☐ | ☐ |
| _____ | ☐ | ☐ | ☐ | ☐ |
| _____ | ☐ | ☐ | ☐ | ☐ |
| _____ | ☐ | ☐ | ☐ | ☐ |
| _____ | ☐ | ☐ | ☐ | ☐ |
| _____ | ☐ | ☐ | ☐ | ☐ |

## Closets

|  | Keep | Toss | Sell | Unsure |
|---|---|---|---|---|
| _____ | ☐ | ☐ | ☐ | ☐ |
| _____ | ☐ | ☐ | ☐ | ☐ |
| _____ | ☐ | ☐ | ☐ | ☐ |
| _____ | ☐ | ☐ | ☐ | ☐ |
| _____ | ☐ | ☐ | ☐ | ☐ |
| _____ | ☐ | ☐ | ☐ | ☐ |
| _____ | ☐ | ☐ | ☐ | ☐ |
| _____ | ☐ | ☐ | ☐ | ☐ |
| _____ | ☐ | ☐ | ☐ | ☐ |
| _____ | ☐ | ☐ | ☐ | ☐ |
| _____ | ☐ | ☐ | ☐ | ☐ |
| _____ | ☐ | ☐ | ☐ | ☐ |
| _____ | ☐ | ☐ | ☐ | ☐ |
| _____ | ☐ | ☐ | ☐ | ☐ |
| _____ | ☐ | ☐ | ☐ | ☐ |
| _____ | ☐ | ☐ | ☐ | ☐ |
| _____ | ☐ | ☐ | ☐ | ☐ |
| _____ | ☐ | ☐ | ☐ | ☐ |

## Closets

<table>
<thead>
<tr><th></th><th>Keep</th><th>Toss</th><th>Sell</th><th>Unsure</th></tr>
</thead>
<tbody>
<tr><td></td><td>☐</td><td>☐</td><td>☐</td><td>☐</td></tr>
<tr><td></td><td>☐</td><td>☐</td><td>☐</td><td>☐</td></tr>
<tr><td></td><td>☐</td><td>☐</td><td>☐</td><td>☐</td></tr>
<tr><td></td><td>☐</td><td>☐</td><td>☐</td><td>☐</td></tr>
<tr><td></td><td>☐</td><td>☐</td><td>☐</td><td>☐</td></tr>
<tr><td></td><td>☐</td><td>☐</td><td>☐</td><td>☐</td></tr>
<tr><td></td><td>☐</td><td>☐</td><td>☐</td><td>☐</td></tr>
<tr><td></td><td>☐</td><td>☐</td><td>☐</td><td>☐</td></tr>
<tr><td></td><td>☐</td><td>☐</td><td>☐</td><td>☐</td></tr>
<tr><td></td><td>☐</td><td>☐</td><td>☐</td><td>☐</td></tr>
<tr><td></td><td>☐</td><td>☐</td><td>☐</td><td>☐</td></tr>
<tr><td></td><td>☐</td><td>☐</td><td>☐</td><td>☐</td></tr>
<tr><td></td><td>☐</td><td>☐</td><td>☐</td><td>☐</td></tr>
<tr><td></td><td>☐</td><td>☐</td><td>☐</td><td>☐</td></tr>
<tr><td></td><td>☐</td><td>☐</td><td>☐</td><td>☐</td></tr>
<tr><td></td><td>☐</td><td>☐</td><td>☐</td><td>☐</td></tr>
<tr><td></td><td>☐</td><td>☐</td><td>☐</td><td>☐</td></tr>
<tr><td></td><td>☐</td><td>☐</td><td>☐</td><td>☐</td></tr>
</tbody>
</table>

## Living Room Furniture

|  | Keep | Toss | Sell | Unsure |
|---|---|---|---|---|
| _____ | ☐ | ☐ | ☐ | ☐ |
| _____ | ☐ | ☐ | ☐ | ☐ |
| _____ | ☐ | ☐ | ☐ | ☐ |
| _____ | ☐ | ☐ | ☐ | ☐ |
| _____ | ☐ | ☐ | ☐ | ☐ |
| _____ | ☐ | ☐ | ☐ | ☐ |
| _____ | ☐ | ☐ | ☐ | ☐ |
| _____ | ☐ | ☐ | ☐ | ☐ |
| _____ | ☐ | ☐ | ☐ | ☐ |
| _____ | ☐ | ☐ | ☐ | ☐ |
| _____ | ☐ | ☐ | ☐ | ☐ |
| _____ | ☐ | ☐ | ☐ | ☐ |
| _____ | ☐ | ☐ | ☐ | ☐ |
| _____ | ☐ | ☐ | ☐ | ☐ |
| _____ | ☐ | ☐ | ☐ | ☐ |
| _____ | ☐ | ☐ | ☐ | ☐ |
| _____ | ☐ | ☐ | ☐ | ☐ |
| _____ | ☐ | ☐ | ☐ | ☐ |

## Living Room Furniture

_____    ☐    ☐    ☐    ☐

_____    ☐    ☐    ☐    ☐

_____    ☐    ☐    ☐    ☐

_____    ☐    ☐    ☐    ☐

_____    ☐    ☐    ☐    ☐

_____    ☐    ☐    ☐    ☐

_____    ☐    ☐    ☐    ☐

_____    ☐    ☐    ☐    ☐

_____    ☐    ☐    ☐    ☐

_____    ☐    ☐    ☐    ☐

_____    ☐    ☐    ☐    ☐

_____    ☐    ☐    ☐    ☐

_____    ☐    ☐    ☐    ☐

_____    ☐    ☐    ☐    ☐

_____    ☐    ☐    ☐    ☐

_____    ☐    ☐    ☐    ☐

_____    ☐    ☐    ☐    ☐

_____    ☐    ☐    ☐    ☐

## Garage/Toolshed

|  | Keep | Toss | Sell | Unsure |
|---|---|---|---|---|
| _____ | ☐ | ☐ | ☐ | ☐ |
| _____ | ☐ | ☐ | ☐ | ☐ |
| _____ | ☐ | ☐ | ☐ | ☐ |
| _____ | ☐ | ☐ | ☐ | ☐ |
| _____ | ☐ | ☐ | ☐ | ☐ |
| _____ | ☐ | ☐ | ☐ | ☐ |
| _____ | ☐ | ☐ | ☐ | ☐ |
| _____ | ☐ | ☐ | ☐ | ☐ |
| _____ | ☐ | ☐ | ☐ | ☐ |
| _____ | ☐ | ☐ | ☐ | ☐ |
| _____ | ☐ | ☐ | ☐ | ☐ |
| _____ | ☐ | ☐ | ☐ | ☐ |
| _____ | ☐ | ☐ | ☐ | ☐ |
| _____ | ☐ | ☐ | ☐ | ☐ |
| _____ | ☐ | ☐ | ☐ | ☐ |
| _____ | ☐ | ☐ | ☐ | ☐ |
| _____ | ☐ | ☐ | ☐ | ☐ |
| _____ | ☐ | ☐ | ☐ | ☐ |

## Garage/Toolshed

| | Keep | Toss | Sell | Unsure |
|---|---|---|---|---|
| _____ | ☐ | ☐ | ☐ | ☐ |
| _____ | ☐ | ☐ | ☐ | ☐ |
| _____ | ☐ | ☐ | ☐ | ☐ |
| _____ | ☐ | ☐ | ☐ | ☐ |
| _____ | ☐ | ☐ | ☐ | ☐ |
| _____ | ☐ | ☐ | ☐ | ☐ |
| _____ | ☐ | ☐ | ☐ | ☐ |
| _____ | ☐ | ☐ | ☐ | ☐ |
| _____ | ☐ | ☐ | ☐ | ☐ |
| _____ | ☐ | ☐ | ☐ | ☐ |
| _____ | ☐ | ☐ | ☐ | ☐ |
| _____ | ☐ | ☐ | ☐ | ☐ |
| _____ | ☐ | ☐ | ☐ | ☐ |
| _____ | ☐ | ☐ | ☐ | ☐ |
| _____ | ☐ | ☐ | ☐ | ☐ |
| _____ | ☐ | ☐ | ☐ | ☐ |
| _____ | ☐ | ☐ | ☐ | ☐ |
| _____ | ☐ | ☐ | ☐ | ☐ |

## Attic/Basement

|  | Keep | Toss | Sell | Unsure |
|---|---|---|---|---|
| _____ | ☐ | ☐ | ☐ | ☐ |
| _____ | ☐ | ☐ | ☐ | ☐ |
| _____ | ☐ | ☐ | ☐ | ☐ |
| _____ | ☐ | ☐ | ☐ | ☐ |
| _____ | ☐ | ☐ | ☐ | ☐ |
| _____ | ☐ | ☐ | ☐ | ☐ |
| _____ | ☐ | ☐ | ☐ | ☐ |
| _____ | ☐ | ☐ | ☐ | ☐ |
| _____ | ☐ | ☐ | ☐ | ☐ |
| _____ | ☐ | ☐ | ☐ | ☐ |
| _____ | ☐ | ☐ | ☐ | ☐ |
| _____ | ☐ | ☐ | ☐ | ☐ |
| _____ | ☐ | ☐ | ☐ | ☐ |
| _____ | ☐ | ☐ | ☐ | ☐ |
| _____ | ☐ | ☐ | ☐ | ☐ |
| _____ | ☐ | ☐ | ☐ | ☐ |
| _____ | ☐ | ☐ | ☐ | ☐ |
| _____ | ☐ | ☐ | ☐ | ☐ |

## Attic/Basement

| | Keep | Toss | Sell | Unsure |
|---|---|---|---|---|
| | ☐ | ☐ | ☐ | ☐ |
| | ☐ | ☐ | ☐ | ☐ |
| | ☐ | ☐ | ☐ | ☐ |
| | ☐ | ☐ | ☐ | ☐ |
| | ☐ | ☐ | ☐ | ☐ |
| | ☐ | ☐ | ☐ | ☐ |
| | ☐ | ☐ | ☐ | ☐ |
| | ☐ | ☐ | ☐ | ☐ |
| | ☐ | ☐ | ☐ | ☐ |
| | ☐ | ☐ | ☐ | ☐ |
| | ☐ | ☐ | ☐ | ☐ |
| | ☐ | ☐ | ☐ | ☐ |
| | ☐ | ☐ | ☐ | ☐ |
| | ☐ | ☐ | ☐ | ☐ |
| | ☐ | ☐ | ☐ | ☐ |
| | ☐ | ☐ | ☐ | ☐ |
| | ☐ | ☐ | ☐ | ☐ |
| | ☐ | ☐ | ☐ | ☐ |

## Artwork

|  | Keep | Toss | Sell | Unsure |
|---|---|---|---|---|
| _____ | ☐ | ☐ | ☐ | ☐ |
| _____ | ☐ | ☐ | ☐ | ☐ |
| _____ | ☐ | ☐ | ☐ | ☐ |
| _____ | ☐ | ☐ | ☐ | ☐ |
| _____ | ☐ | ☐ | ☐ | ☐ |
| _____ | ☐ | ☐ | ☐ | ☐ |
| _____ | ☐ | ☐ | ☐ | ☐ |
| _____ | ☐ | ☐ | ☐ | ☐ |
| _____ | ☐ | ☐ | ☐ | ☐ |
| _____ | ☐ | ☐ | ☐ | ☐ |
| _____ | ☐ | ☐ | ☐ | ☐ |
| _____ | ☐ | ☐ | ☐ | ☐ |
| _____ | ☐ | ☐ | ☐ | ☐ |
| _____ | ☐ | ☐ | ☐ | ☐ |
| _____ | ☐ | ☐ | ☐ | ☐ |
| _____ | ☐ | ☐ | ☐ | ☐ |
| _____ | ☐ | ☐ | ☐ | ☐ |
| _____ | ☐ | ☐ | ☐ | ☐ |

## Jewelry

| | Keep | Toss | Sell | Unsure |
|---|---|---|---|---|
| | ☐ | ☐ | ☐ | ☐ |
| | ☐ | ☐ | ☐ | ☐ |
| | ☐ | ☐ | ☐ | ☐ |
| | ☐ | ☐ | ☐ | ☐ |
| | ☐ | ☐ | ☐ | ☐ |
| | ☐ | ☐ | ☐ | ☐ |
| | ☐ | ☐ | ☐ | ☐ |
| | ☐ | ☐ | ☐ | ☐ |
| | ☐ | ☐ | ☐ | ☐ |
| | ☐ | ☐ | ☐ | ☐ |
| | ☐ | ☐ | ☐ | ☐ |
| | ☐ | ☐ | ☐ | ☐ |
| | ☐ | ☐ | ☐ | ☐ |
| | ☐ | ☐ | ☐ | ☐ |
| | ☐ | ☐ | ☐ | ☐ |
| | ☐ | ☐ | ☐ | ☐ |
| | ☐ | ☐ | ☐ | ☐ |
| | ☐ | ☐ | ☐ | ☐ |

**Other**

|  | Keep | Toss | Sell | Unsure |
|---|---|---|---|---|
| _____ | ☐ | ☐ | ☐ | ☐ |
| _____ | ☐ | ☐ | ☐ | ☐ |
| _____ | ☐ | ☐ | ☐ | ☐ |
| _____ | ☐ | ☐ | ☐ | ☐ |
| _____ | ☐ | ☐ | ☐ | ☐ |
| _____ | ☐ | ☐ | ☐ | ☐ |
| _____ | ☐ | ☐ | ☐ | ☐ |
| _____ | ☐ | ☐ | ☐ | ☐ |
| _____ | ☐ | ☐ | ☐ | ☐ |
| _____ | ☐ | ☐ | ☐ | ☐ |
| _____ | ☐ | ☐ | ☐ | ☐ |
| _____ | ☐ | ☐ | ☐ | ☐ |
| _____ | ☐ | ☐ | ☐ | ☐ |
| _____ | ☐ | ☐ | ☐ | ☐ |
| _____ | ☐ | ☐ | ☐ | ☐ |
| _____ | ☐ | ☐ | ☐ | ☐ |
| _____ | ☐ | ☐ | ☐ | ☐ |
| _____ | ☐ | ☐ | ☐ | ☐ |

## OUCH! THIS STUFF HURTS

The range of emotions we feel when we're downsizing runs the gamut from hilarity and revelation to melancholy and grief. Rather than dodge these very human reactions, acknowledge them. Write down what you experienced as you sorted the following. Include fond memories that surfaced, as well as funny ones.

》 When I went through the clothes . . .

_____

_____

_____

_____

_____

_____

》 When I went through the kitchen . . .

_____

_____

_____

_____

_____

❯ When I went through the garage/toolshed . . .

_____

_____

_____

_____

_____

_____

_____

❯ When I went through the closets . . .

_____

_____

_____

_____

_____

_____

_____

❯ When I went through the artwork . . .

_____

_____

_____

_____

_____

_____

_____

❯ When I went through the attic/basement . . .

_____

_____

_____

_____

_____

_____

_____

❯ When I went through the furniture . . .

_____

_____

_____

_____

_____

_____

_____

❯ When I went through the  _____

_____

_____

_____

_____

_____

_____

_____

7

# Downsizing with Siblings

Siblings don't always agree on how to divide a loved one's belongings. Arguments are unfortunately common. But many families come up with fair ways to successfully divide belongings to achieve a harmonious outcome.

In *Downsizing the Family Home*, we met three siblings, adult children working together to clear out the family home after both their parents had died. "There were some arguments," said Peter, one of the siblings. "We fought . . . because of the emotional weight of sorting through it all."

Peter told me, for instance, that he wanted the family's two antique clocks, and so did his sisters. When this became contentious, Peter said he did some soul searching. What mattered, he realized, was not that he had both these clocks in his house. (He now has one.) "What I really wanted was to keep them in the family," he said.

I felt the same way about an oil painting of a seascape that used to hang over my parents' fireplace. I loved that painting and would have found a place for it in my home, but when I saw my brother had hung it over his stairs in his house, that was even better.

The key here is that every family has to resolve the distribution of household furnishings in a way that works for them. Take time to talk the process through so all agree.

❯ Here's how my family members and I agreed to divide the homestead:

_____

_____

_____

_____

_____

_____

_____

_____

_____

_____

_____

_____

_____

_____

_____

_____

❭ We all wanted the _____, so here's how we handled it:

_____

_____

_____

_____

_____

_____

_____

_____

_____

_____

_____

_____

_____

_____

_____

_____

❯ It was important to me that I got these items, which I did, because . . .

_____

_____

_____

_____

_____

_____

❯ Here's how I felt when someone else got what I wanted:

_____

_____

_____

_____

_____

_____

❯ List who in your family received other key belongings to keep a record of what items were kept in the family.

_____

_____

_____

_____

_____

_____

_____

_____

_____

_____

_____

_____

_____

❯ What causes or charities did my donations benefit? These could be animal or women's shelters, churches or temples, veterans groups, etc.

_____

_____

_____

_____

_____

_____

_____

_____

_____

_____

_____

_____

8

# Ready, Set, Sell!

Now that you have singled out what you are selling, ask yourself what kind of sale you want to have. It helps to know the lingo:

- **ESTATE SALE.** Though it sounds fitting for a grand mansion behind gates, an estate sale simply means a whole household of goods is on sale, regardless of how modest the abode might be. It usually features more and better items than yard or garage sales and is typically held indoors.

- **GARAGE, MOVING, OR YARD SALE.** This is when a person is cleaning house and putting items on the driveway, in the yard, and in the garage for sale.

- **RUMMAGE SALE.** This is an invitation for buyers to dig through an unorganized mound and look for buried treasure.

 INSIDE TIP: *Local sites such as Craigslist are perfect for large items, such as furniture, that buyers can pick up. Online auction sites such as eBay are good places to sell smaller, more valuable items, such as collectibles and fine jewelry, which are easy to ship.*

▶ **ONLINE SALE.** Craigslist and other classified sites are like online yard sales, perfect if you want fast cash and don't want to host a sale or pay someone else to sell your stuff. With Craigslist or other neighborhood sites, buyers tend to be local, so you avoid shipping costs. Online auction sites, such as eBay, can attract buyers from around the world, widening your reach but often requiring shipping.

As you plan your sale, consider the following suggestions:

## Estate, Garage, and Other Sales

▶ **SET A DAY AND TIME FOR THE SALE.** Weekends will draw more crowds. However, weekdays tend to draw professional buyers.

▶ **ADVERTISE YOUR EVENT.** Place online ads for your sale on sites such as EstateSales.net, PennySaver.com, and Craigslist; and post signs around the neighborhood.

▶ **RESEARCH PRICES ONLINE.** Check sites like eBay and Craigslist to see what similar items are selling for before pricing them for sale.

▶ **FIND THE PAPERWORK.** If you plan to sell artwork or other fine collectibles, organize certificates of authenticity and research information about the artist and the piece you're selling so you can justify its value to prospective buyers.

▶ **GET CHANGE.** This is a cash business. You do not want to take personal checks. Be ready to make change.

▶ **GET HELP.** Enlist friends or relatives. You don't want to do this alone.

## Online Sales

▶ **SET UP ACCOUNTS.** Sign up for accounts on sites such as Craigslist and eBay. Accept only cash in person from Craigslist buyers. Watch out for scams, which are plentiful. For sites like eBay, which involve shipping goods, you'll want to establish an account with PayPal or a similar service that protects both buyers and sellers. Note listing and other fees charged by these sites.

▶ **RESEARCH PRICES.** Check competitive listings to see what similar items have sold for before pricing them for sale. (Ignore list prices, which are meaningless.)

▶ **PREPARE YOUR ITEMS FOR SALE.** Photograph each item from several angles, making sure to polish jewelry and light it well. Include an honest description, with the item's measurements if applicable. (For more tips for selling online, see Chapter 9 of *Downsizing the Family Home.*)

INSIDE TIP: *When valuing art, keep in mind two kinds of value: objective value, what it truly is worth on the market, and subjective value, how much it is worth to you. Market value will depend on how well-known the artist is, whether the art is original or signed, and its rarity and size. What a piece is worth to you will depend on how well it works with your furnishings and its sentimental value, which may be priceless.*

## Specialty Items

▶ **CONSULT AN APPRAISER.** Everyone wants to be that buyer who finds the dusty Rembrandt at a garage sale for $100. But no one wants to be that seller. If your family has items you believe or suspect to be of high worth—such as antique handwoven rugs, original paintings from known artists, Chippendale chairs, vintage jewelry or watches from known makers—find an appraiser experienced in the genre. You should also have rare books, collectible coins, and comic books appraised before you set a selling price.

▶ **PULL OUT AUCTION AND CONSIGNMENT ITEMS.** If in fact you have any high-end antiques or collectibles, you might want to consult an auction house. Items of lesser value, but still of some worth, might best be taken to an antique or furniture consignment store in town, which usually will give you between 40 and 60 percent of the sales price.

▶ **KNOW YOUR NET.** Auction houses typically take 10 to 15 percent. Find out what the house's take is up front and where it will place the starting bid. The same holds for consignment shops.

**9**

# What I Sold Where

Perhaps the most rewarding part of holding an estate or garage sale for a family household is the quick cash you can collect. Cash can soothe the sting of loss, furnish a new place, or—as in my case, clearing out my parents' house and selling it—go toward paying for long-term care. Such garage and estate sales are sobering, though, because they reveal what belongings are really worth—generally, a lot less than we think.

 INSIDE TIP: *As hard as it can be, try to separate sentimental value from market value. This is a time to be practical.*

## FOR THE RECORD

Keeping a record of what sold, for how much, and to whom—along with an occasional photo—can serve as both a reference and a memento. When months later you feel a wistful pang, you can look back and see what something was worth, have a record as a piece of family history, and imagine where it might be now.

Use the space on the following pages to record details of items sold at estate sales, auctions, consignment shops, and online.

| Item for Sale | Where Sold/To Whom | Amount Received |
|---------------|--------------------|-----------------|
|               |                    |                 |
|               |                    |                 |
|               |                    |                 |
|               |                    |                 |
|               |                    |                 |
|               |                    |                 |
|               |                    |                 |
|               |                    |                 |
|               |                    |                 |
|               |                    |                 |
|               |                    |                 |
|               |                    |                 |
|               |                    |                 |
|               |                    |                 |
|               |                    |                 |
|               |                    |                 |
|               |                    |                 |
|               |                    |                 |

| Item for Sale | Where Sold/To Whom | Amount Received |
| --- | --- | --- |
| | | |
| | | |
| | | |
| | | |
| | | |
| | | |
| | | |
| | | |
| | | |
| | | |
| | | |
| | | |
| | | |
| | | |
| | | |
| | | |
| | | |
| | | |
| | | |

| Item for Sale | Where Sold/To Whom | Amount Received |
|---|---|---|
| | | |
| | | |
| | | |
| | | |
| | | |
| | | |
| | | |
| | | |
| | | |
| | | |
| | | |
| | | |
| | | |
| | | |
| | | |
| | | |
| | | |
| | | |

| Item for Sale | Where Sold/To Whom | Amount Received |
|---|---|---|
| | | |
| | | |
| | | |
| | | |
| | | |
| | | |
| | | |
| | | |
| | | |
| | | |
| | | |
| | | |
| | | |
| | | |
| | | |
| | | |
| | | |
| | | |

❯ It's easy to believe cherished belongings are worth more than they are, but the value of these items surprised me:

_____

_____

_____

_____

_____

To remember these items, paste a photograph in the area below.

## BE A BLESSING, NOT A BURDEN

Of course, the tendency is to want to keep treasured possessions in the family. The problem is, sometimes family members don't want what you treasure. Just because you saved Johnny's Cub Scout uniform so he could have it someday doesn't guarantee he'll want it. Remember the snowball effect, and let your legacy be to help members of the next generation keep their footprints light.

❯ List here what family members said they wanted, and what they ultimately took, even if they took nothing (which is fine, by the way).

_____

_____

_____

_____

_____

_____

_____

_____

_____

_____

If you would like, include photos in the space below of items taken by family members.

## 10

# The Gift of Giving

As we go through life, most of us come to care about a cause, either because of its impact on us or a loved one, or because we believe the mission is important. Many believe leaving a legacy is part of living a full life. Whether it's a shelter for the homeless or for battered women, or an organization that protects animals, or a group that advocates for a cause you believe in, look into how you might donate your items to help others, or donate items to a cause your loved one cared about.

When clearing out my parents' home, I took a bundle of blankets and towels to a local animal rescue. When my husband and I got married two years ago and blended two fully loaded households, we had a lot of redundant furniture and housewares. Fortunately for my oldest daughter, who had just graduated from college and was setting up her first apartment, we gave her a great start. With what remained, we filled a trailer truck and dropped off our donations at the Sharing Center, which provides resources to people in need in our community.

Donating to such centers is a win-win. You get a tax write-off, but mostly you get a good feeling knowing that you are helping others.

❯ What causes did your loved one value? Which ones do you value?
How did you contribute through your donation?

_____

_____

_____

_____

_____

_____

_____

_____

_____

_____

_____

_____

_____

_____

❱ Itemize particularly special donations, such as donating a car to the Red Cross.

❱ *I felt good donating* _____

   *to* _____

   *because* _____.


❱ *I felt good donating* _____

   *to* _____

   *because* _____.


❱ *I felt good donating* _____

   *to* _____

   *because* _____.


❱ *I felt good donating* _____

   *to* _____

   *because* _____.


❱ *I felt good donating* _____

   *to* _____

   *because* _____.

❯ Just because you've donated a special item doesn't mean it can't live in your memory.

Include photos of meaningful donated items in the space below.

## 11

# Then the Going Got Tough

As you work your way through belongings, sorting them into piles—toss, sell or donate, and keep—you inevitably have a fourth pile. It's the "I don't know" pile, which I refer to as the pile of postponement. You're plowing along pretty well, and then you hit a box of your parents' love letters, or your mom's wedding dress, or your kids' kindergarten art, or some military memorabilia, or old photos. You come to a halt, and rightly so. These items deserve special consideration.

This is your chance to create your family museum, a well-edited collection of mementos that concisely reflect and preserve the family history. These items really seem like the stuff of life. But volume is still a problem. Your task is to figure out how to preserve these memories with an economy of space. Put important medals in a frame under glass. Scan love letters and photos. Use the fabric from a special dress to make something small, like a sachet. Or, give the object its due, and let it go.

INSIDE TIP: *Pass it down, but differently. When I remarried recently, I took pieces from my mother's wedding dress and used the fabric to wrap the bouquets that my two daughters and I carried. Look for opportunities to pay tradition forward, in small but symbolic ways.*

> What is in my pile of postponement?

_____

_____

_____

_____

_____

_____

_____

_____

_____

_____

_____

_____

_____

_____

❯ Why are these items so loaded?

_____

_____

_____

_____

_____

_____

❯ What are my options?

_____

_____

_____

_____

_____

_____

*"Take time to deliberate, but when the time for action comes, stop thinking and go in."*

—NAPOLEON BONAPARTE

❭ Here's what I decided to do with the really tough stuff:

*The wedding dress . . .*

_____

_____

_____

_____

_____

_____

**Attach a photo below.**

*The love letters . . .*

_____

_____

_____

_____

_____

_____

**Attach a photo below.**

*The military memorabilia . . .*

_____

_____

_____

_____

_____

_____

**Attach a photo below.**

*The family photos . . .*

_____

_____

_____

_____

_____

_____

**Attach a special photo below.**

*Other . . .*

_____

_____

_____

_____

_____

_____

**Attach a special photo below.**

❯ *I really wanted to keep* _____ ,

   *but I didn't because* _____

   _____

   _____


❯ *Instead I kept* _____

   _____

   _____


❯ *We found many pictures of* _____ ,

   *but I chose to save this one because:* _____

   _____

   _____


**Attach a photo below.**

# 12

# Collections Are a Special Case

Collections pose a challenge to those trying to respect the family museum. Many believe we must keep collections intact to retain their value or to respect the collector. Experts will assure you, however, that most collections are not worth more combined than as separate collectibles—in general, by selling prize items individually, you will receive more than if you sell off the collection as a whole. So you now have their permission to dissolve the collection, and sell one collectible at a time.

Here are more ways we can keep the past present, but smaller. If someone had a collection, say, of antique cameras or English teapots, then save one, or three, and sell the rest. Keep photos of them all if you like, but a sampling will preserve the essence—minus the bulk. My mother collected beautiful handkerchiefs. She had dozens. I saved one for myself and one for each of my daughters. That is enough.

 To honor my loved one's collection of _____ , here's what I did:

_____

_____

_____

_____

_____

_____

_____

❯ Here is a photo of the collection (or special pieces I did not keep):

# A Word to Collectors: Don't Keep It Together

I once spoke to a woman who told me that she and her husband, both pharmacists, had a plan. They had amassed a collection of mortars and pestles from around the world. When they died, they wanted these sets distributed at their funeral as favors, which may strike you as a little odd. But, hey, it's their funeral.

Initially, I thought she should not break up the collection but rather donate it intact to, say, a pharmacy school. It turns out her instincts were better than mine.

In researching this further, I learned that I was confusing collections with sets. The two compilations merit different treatment.

My instinct to keep the collection of mortars and pestles together stemmed from an incident that happened in my family. When my grandmother died, my oldest cousin divvied up place settings of my grandmother's china among the family members. I got two place settings of the old-fashioned flowered, ruffle-bordered china, which I didn't want. I have china. I also have my mother's china. I loved Grandma Mac—but her china, not so much.

I accepted it graciously, of course, and tucked the china in a closet. My brother also got two sets and was at a loss. He and his wife had their own china, in addition to her mother's. He tactfully suggested that my cousin give the china to someone else in the family who might appreciate it more.

Feelings got hurt. I received phone calls and played family referee, balancing my cousin's good intentions with my brother's desire to reunite the collection—elsewhere.

My belief that the set of china was better together than divided influenced my advice to the mortar and pestle collector.

A collections expert from Heritage Auctions, the largest auction house founded in the United States, straightened me out.

While sets—like china—are better intact, "almost every collection is worth more broken up," said Heritage co-owner Jim Halperin. "Although every collector's dream is to leave their collection intact the way they envisioned it, that's almost always a complete fantasy."

Halperin says he, too, dreams of selling his collections intact, "but I purge that from my mind."

*Continued*

Then he cleared up a few more collection myths; these questions and answers may help you decide how and where to let go:

▶ *What is a collectible?* Collectibles are items like coins, stamps, and sports cars, made in quantity but now rare and thus desired.

▶ *What is the difference between a collector and a hoarder?* Collectors study and know everything about what they collect. They track what they have, know what they want, have a plan, and organize systematically, cataloging items. Hoarders acquire without direction and don't throw anything away.

▶ *What is the best way to profit from a collection?* When you have a group of distinct items, such as original hand-drawn cartoon animation cels (a cel, short for celluloid, is a transparent sheet on which objects are drawn or painted for traditional, hand-drawn animation), you will almost always get more by selling one at a time, either at an auction or through eBay. That is your best chance of finding a collector looking for that specific item.

▶ *What if the whole collection is "museum worthy"?* Even so, museums will likely only want a few pieces. They don't have the room to display it all, and the extra pieces clog up their basements. "If you really want to help the museum," Halperin advises, "let museum officials pick what they want to display, and then sell the rest and give them the money. Even museums would rather have money than art."

▶ *How should you dispose of a collection?* Collectors should arrange to sell items in their collection one at a time and not leave their family members stuck selling valuables they don't know about or appreciate.

The pharmacists had the right idea, after all.

# PART FOUR

# Keepsake

What we choose to keep is made more precious by what we don't save. My list of keepsakes from my family home is not long: my mother's pearls, her French coin purse, one of her lace handkerchiefs (plus one each for my daughters), two oil paintings, three crystal Lalique birds, the china, the silver, my father's cigar box, and his military medals. Those are the treasures I kept—those, and a heart full of memories.

# 13

# The Treasure Hunt

One way to honor and remember your loved one is to go on a treasure hunt. If it's your loved one's home, choose the five (or maybe a few more) items that give you a warm connection to them but that don't result in clutter. If it's your home, you can also apply this method to your pile of postponement. I picked a few items I knew my mother loved, and that I loved, too, including an oil painting that had hung in our kitchen—and now hangs in mine. It's a nice connection. That and a few more keepsakes are really enough. The less you have, the more it means. Hold on only to what makes your heart sing.

 INSIDE TIP: *Rather than decide what to get rid of, instead choose what to keep. Take everything out of a space, and then pretend you're shopping. What would you buy again? Acquiring instead of giving up is psychologically much more rewarding.*

》 I went on a treasure hunt. Here's what I saved and why:

_____

_____

_____

❯ Attach photos of treasures you saved, and those special items you ultimately decided to let go of. Be sure to include captions indicating what you saved and what you sold or donated.

_____

_____

_____

14

# Rightsizing Our Memories

The problem with saving stuff is that it takes up room—room we often can't spare or afford. Yes, I'm talking about those storage units you are paying for, the garages you can't park in, the rooms and closets you can't use because they are stuffed with stuff, and the attics so loaded they are ready to bring down the house. A better plan is to save the memory and not the item by literally paring it down to size. For instance, using pinking shears, snip a swatch from a dress, blouse, apron, or baby blanket. Then paste it on the pages that follow, and write down when it was worn or used and why you remember it fondly. This way, you can capture the memory in a tangible way, and free up the space the garments consumed.

INSIDE TIP: *The statistics are sobering: According to a 2015 survey from Sparefoot.com, there were more storage facilities in the United States than there were Starbucks™, McDonald's®, and Subway® restaurants combined. We have 53,000 storage facilities, according to the national Self Storage Association, and they are more than 90 percent full. The average cost of storage is $125 a month for a 10-by-10, non-climate-controlled locker. That comes to $1,500 a year. Do not become the one out of every ten households that rents a storage unit. Let go, and lighten up.*

## SAVE A REMNANT

On the next several pages, use the prompts to create a scrapbook—a collage of fabrics and photos with captions.

❯ Snip a swatch of fabric from a dress worn at a special occasion, such as a birthday or anniversary, and glue or paste it next to a photo from the event.

**Attach your swatch here.**

**Attach your photo here.**

Caption _____

_____

_____

❯ Clip a piece of an apron that belonged to the chef in the family, and place it here along with his or her most famous recipe.

Attach your swatch here.

Recipe

_____

_____

_____

_____

_____

_____

_____

_____

_____

_____

❯ Clip a swatch from a favorite cowboy shirt, fishing vest, or other garment associated with a beloved hobby, and attach it with a corresponding photo of a favorite horse, fishing hole, and so on.

Attach your swatch here.

Attach your photo here.

Caption _____

_____

_____

❯ Snip a piece of a baby bib or blanket, and pair it with a photo of the child to whom it belonged.

Attach your swatch here.

Attach your photo here.

Caption _____

_____

_____

❱ Tell your own fabric story.

Attach your fabric here.

**The fabric story.**

_____

_____

_____

_____

_____

_____

_____

_____

_____

_____

## REPURPOSE WITH PURPOSE

Besides saving a remnant, or a sample, another way to make the past present or to honor a loved one is to take items and repurpose them. I've heard from readers who turned a vintage wedding dress into a christening gown, or into pillows. After her father died, one woman took his large collection of lovely silk neckties and had a quilter weave them into a three-foot-square quilt, creating a beautiful wall hanging that is now a family heirloom. Another downsizer took pieces of her mom's colorful china, had it crushed, and turned it into mosaic trivets that she shared among family members.

> How can or did you repurpose your loved one's items while making them smaller and more useful?

_____

_____

_____

_____

_____

_____

_____

_____

_____

## Keep Those Who Have Passed Present, Beautifully

A book about ways to turn your deceased loved one's belongings into tangible mementos first struck me as misguided. After all, I favor letting go, and not bogging down the present with the stuff of the past.

But *Passed and Present: Keeping Memories of Loved Ones Alive*, by Allison Gilbert changed my view. She managed to strike that sweet spot of memorializing loved ones in tasteful, clutter-free ways.

"Of course, we yearn to have them with us," said Gilbert in an interview I had with her. Gilbert has also lost both of her parents. "But keeping their memory alive is the next best way of keeping those who have passed present.

"Possessions quickly become clutter if you're not selective," she said. "The real joy comes from how you elevate one or two items that your loved one cherished, and how that evokes that person and keeps their story present."

For instance, her grandmother was a knitter. Gilbert said she made "lots of ugly sweaters for all her family members, which they never wore." They hogged space and did not create feelings of endearment. Then Gilbert had a thought. She gathered all the sweaters, unraveled them, and had mittens made from the yarn. "We got rid of the bulk, and got back a useful asset and a story that lets us remember Grandma more positively." Now that's a great idea: smaller, useful, and meaningful.

Here are a few more ways to keep those who have passed present:

- ▶ **REPURPOSE.** Have an old leather jacket remade into a useful tote.

- ▶ **INITIAL HERE.** Find a sample of your loved one's handwriting and isolate a section, such as "Love, Pete." Take the written words to a jeweler to have them emblazoned or etched on a charm or cufflinks.

- ▶ **SMASH THE CHINA.** Take pieces to a jeweler or crafter who can turn china plates into tiered cake stands. My favorite idea is to smash the china and use the shards to create mosaic trivets, trays, planters, or frames, which also make good family gifts.

- ▶ **FRAME THEM IN ACTION.** Elevate a loved one's interest: Feature a photo of a gardener in her garden, alongside a seed packet or a pressed flower. Place a photo of Grandpa's horse alongside a fragment of a rein.

> How did repurposing the items help you appreciate them?

_____

_____

_____

_____

_____

_____

_____

_____

_____

_____

_____

_____

_____

_____

_____

❯ The new items fit better in my life because . . .

_____

_____

_____

_____

_____

_____

_____

_____

_____

_____

_____

_____

_____

_____

_____

*"Things are only worth
what you make them worth."*

——MOLIÈRE

**Attach a photo of the original item here.**

**Attach a photo of the newly repurposed item here.**

# PART FIVE

# Homestead

Whenever I'm in towns where I used to live, I can't resist driving by my old homes. The home I grew up in, where my parents lived for nearly fifty years, evokes powerful feelings of nostalgia. When I drive by, I can still see them standing outside the front door waving at me, a dog at their feet. The home where I married the father of my children and brought home my two babies has a similar tug on my heart, as do the homes where the kids grew up. These are my anchors, and theirs. To me, they represent chapters of my life. I feel as if I am etched in their walls. When I drive by, I pull over and sit out front for a few minutes and look. As I do, I feel as if I'm opening an old, favorite book and reliving the stories. Before I drive away, I take a moment to thank the house for the shelter it gave me, and for its embrace.

## 15

# Learning the Meaning of Home

Gone but not forgotten. That's the thought we hold when we lose a loved one or move from a house full of memories. Shortly after my mom died, I asked a grief counselor how people in this situation get through the sadness. "It helps to look at the significance of her life," the counselor told me. I used that premise to write my mother's eulogy. I talked about how she honored her Scottish heritage, and how she served her country as a nurse during World War II, her community as a public school nurse and active church member, and her family as a dedicated wife and mother.

Taking the time to think about and record the significance of my mom's life, and what she taught me about the meaning of home, helped me move through my grief. The same held true for my dad, who died a few years before Mom. Some of the best advice I got about life he dispensed in the garage, while he worked on cars and I sat nearby. Though always car related, the advice had broader applications:

- Turn off your radio once in a while and listen.
- Always keep your eye on your pressures and your treads.
- Watch the car that's two cars ahead of you.
- Drive in the center lane so you have two ways out.
- Steer clear of cars with dents and out-of-state plates.
- Don't run the air when you can put the windows down.

His words are part of my memories of home. We all have special memories of our homes, and lessons we learned there. Thus, when we downsize our homes—places where we have lived, learned, and loved—to move on to new chapters, we need to pause. It's important to take a moment to reflect—to honor and thank the home for what it has meant to us, and the people we shared it with—to acknowledge our gratitude for them and their meaning in our lives.

❭ If you're downsizing the home of a loved one, think about the significance of this person's life. What did he or she teach you?

_____

_____

_____

_____

_____

_____

_____

_____

_____

_____

How would this person want to be remembered?

_____

_____

_____

_____

_____

_____

_____

How would you like to honor your loved one's memory?

_____

_____

_____

_____

_____

_____

_____

> What room do you most associate with your loved one? Write about your memories of the person in that space.

## Mom and Home: A Tribute

"Your mom has gone home," the nurse told me, when my mother died, at age ninety-four.

Mom. Gone. Home.

I tried to absorb those three words together. See, two of those words, Mom and home, were as interwoven as sunlight and air. What was new and hard to incorporate was gone.

Like many mothers, my mom defined home, taught me its meaning, and infused my sense of the word.

The day mom died, a grief counselor told me, "There's no closer relationship than the one between mother and child. We're not just connected to our mothers, we're enmeshed."

"How do you get through this?" I asked.

"It helps to look at the significance of her life."

By example, Mom showed me how to have a career and a family, and do both well. She taught me that a woman should have a soft heart, a firm handshake, a quick smile, a slow temper, an easy laugh, a straight spine, regular hair appointments, a signature fragrance, a strong faith, clear opinions, clean linens, something intelligent to read, something intelligent to say, a constructive purpose, and the ability to transform into a defensive lineman should anyone threaten her family.

Mom also taught me how to make a home—not so much what a home should look like, but what it should feel like, which matters more. The home I grew up in was so welcoming, my friends used to stop by even when I wasn't there and long after I had moved out.

Because of my mom, I learned that home is . . .

. . . where you can arrive at any hour and they will take you in.

. . . where predictable patterns—in my case, the smell of coffee in the morning, a dog asleep on the cool tile by the front door, birds at the bird feeder, roses from the garden on the table, and a full cookie jar—assure you that whatever happens out there, life is safe in here.

. . . where your loved ones will listen to your half-baked ideas, and tell you in no uncertain terms what they think about them.

. . . where someone will hang your goofy art and awkward photos on the fridge.

. . . where family and friends sit around the dinner table and talk.

. . . where you can find food for your body, mind, and soul.

. . . where coffee and conversation can resolve almost any problem.

. . . where you can let your hair down, prop your feet up, take your armor off, put your pajamas on, and drop your cares at the door.

Beyond the meaning of home, Mom also taught me this: When facing a tough situation, the best way out is through.

〉 Write a tribute to the person or people who taught you the meaning of home.

_____

_____

_____

_____

_____

_____

_____

_____

16

# How to Say Good-Bye to a House

"Congratulations on your new house," I heard the escrow officer say—not to me. I was the seller. I had moved out of the home six years earlier and had been renting it out until this day came. Nonetheless, the simple comment made me freeze, as I weathered a flood of feelings, both celebratory and sad.

My emotions were mixed, because I was saying good-bye to a house I had designed every inch of. I'd watched the workers build the big brown stucco and stone Colorado house. I'd handpicked every detail and finish. I raised my two daughters there for eight years—eight first days of school, eight Christmases, dozens of birthdays, and thousands of dinners, bedtime stories, and friends coming and going. And then one went off to college, and the other moved to a new state with me, as I said good-bye to an era and a house when a long marriage sadly unwound.

That simple "congratulations" marked the first moment in fourteen years that I was no longer financially responsible for that house. In that instant, a weight lifted, a mortgage fell away, a title changed hands, and a wistfulness rose in my chest.

It is possible to want something that makes you sad. And that was it, a moment I had long waited for, come and gone.

I reached over, shook the new owners' hands, and told them I was glad my house was going to a good home. I had moved on. In the intervening years, I had started a new life, embarked on a new marriage, and bought a new house, all of which I very much loved.

Afterward, I drove by the old, brown house to say good-bye and pay homage to a chapter of my life. I sat out front for a few minutes and felt as if I were opening an old, favorite book. I saw the built-in barbecue out back and thought of the family cookouts. I could picture the dogs on the deck and the kids coming home from school, their backpacks left at the door. A wave of nostalgia washed over me.

Although I know houses are mere structures on land, I can never feel indifferent about houses in which I've lived. They keep my memories in their vaults. Whenever I leave a house, I take a little piece with me, something inconspicuous—a piece of stone, an old knob, a piece of trim—as a keepsake. I keep it along with a journal like this one, with pictures of the house. I do this for my soul.

Before I drove away that day, I thanked the house for the shelter it had provided my family, for hosting the many celebrations, and for holding us close.

I share this remembrance because feelings of grief as you let go of a home are natural. We leave a piece of ourselves in every home in which we've lived. To fail to acknowledge this fact is to fail to understand the meaning of home, and, I would add, to fail to be human.

❯ What does the home you're in today mean to you?

_____

_____

_____

_____

_____

_____

_____

_____

_____

_____

_____

_____

_____

_____

_____

❯ What would you like your children or grandchildren to inherit from this home's meaning?

_____

_____

_____

_____

_____

_____

_____

_____

_____

_____

_____

_____

_____

_____

_____

❯ My home is the place where . . .

_____

_____

_____

_____

_____

_____

_____

_____

_____

_____

_____

_____

_____

_____

_____

_____

_____

---

---

---

---

---

---

---

---

---

---

---

---

---

---

---

---

---

❯ Years from now, I hope my children think about their family home and remember . . .

_____

_____

_____

_____

_____

_____

_____

_____

_____

_____

_____

_____

_____

❭ Honor your home as you leave it, by writing a letter.

*Dear Home:*

_____

_____

_____

_____

_____

_____

_____

_____

_____

_____

_____

_____

_____

_____

*"We leave behind
a bit of ourselves
wherever we have been."*

——EDMOND HARAUCOURT

**A Final Thought**

# It's About Time

As you come to the end of your downsizing journey, my hope is that this workbook has supported you and guided you while you sorted, sold, remembered, and reflected. I hope it provided companionship, courage, and clarity as you purged, streamlined, and cherished what was—and what is.

Beyond that, my wish for all of us completing our downsizing journeys is that we have what we need, and no more—that our hearts are full and our homes are pared to the essentials. That we are not leaving a burden for the next generation, but rather bestowing the gift of having put order in our lives, so they don't have to. That we have appreciated and payed forward the true meaning of home.

I promise, your successors would much rather have what you've captured in this book—your downsizing story—than the headache of clearing out the contents of a home, or, heaven forbid, a storage unit.

That is the legacy of a thoughtful, responsible life.

And there's one more truth to consider: Yes, it's hard to let go of our things or those of a loved one, because we endow them with meaning. But there is another reason we cling. It's about time. Try as we might, we cannot stop time. Sorting through old wedding pictures, baby mementos, school diplomas, and career accolades is a flashflood reminder that life is passing. Holding on to the material world will not make time stand still. Life moves on whether we keep up with the stream, or stay stuck, tethered to an old moss rock.

I hope this workbook has freed you to move on. If I have held the torch for you, and helped light your way, then that has been my profound privilege. Now the torch is yours to carry. Use it to light the way for the next generation. Show them how to live in the present, not the past, and move unencumbered into the future.

And remind them, as you now know, what ultimately matters is who we are, not what we have, and what is to come, not what has been. The time is now. Live well.

"The greatest wealth is
to live content with little."

——PLATO

# Acknowledgments

For the fact that this book is in your hands, a team of talented publishing experts deserves recognition. Though authors get the cover credit, these gifted individuals are the scaffolding on which all this hangs.

My heartfelt appreciation thus goes to my agent Linda Konner, who sees farther than I; my editor on this project, Meredith Hale, by whom no detail slips; Barbara Berger, who edited the parent book and channeled the inspiration for this workbook; Jodi Lipson, Director of AARP Books; and all those at AARP who champion the need to help folks through the essential downsizing process.

For their technical and artistic contributions, I am grateful to the workbook's designer Barbara Balch, interior art director Christine Heun, production editor Michael Cea, jacket designer David Ter-Avanesyan, copy editor Judi Gaelick, proofreader Lisa Geller, production manager Terence Campo, and, of course, to Sterling Publishing.

In addition, none of this would have happened without the continued support of the truly dear readers and editors of my weekly column "At Home With Marni Jameson."

Finally, and not least, I am eternally grateful for those who shore me up on the home front: my daughters Paige and Marissa, and the ever-patient and supportive Doug Carey. My love for you knows no bounds.

# Sources

WWW.SELFSTORAGE.ORG (The Self Storage Association) (for survey cited on page 109, *see* "2015–16 Self Storage Industry Fact Sheet," July 1, 2015, http://www.selfstorage.org/ portals/0/Library/Public Library/Preamble and Fact Sheet (2015) July 2015.pdf)

WWW.SPAREFOOT.COM (SpareFoot blog) (for survey cited on page 109, see John Egan, "Guess How Many U.S. Storage Facilities There Are Versus Subway, McDonald's and Starbucks," May 11, 2015, https://www.sparefoot.com/self-storage/blog/7775-how-many-storage-facilities-are-in-the-us/)

# AARP

**AARP.ORG/BOOKSTORE:** AARP print and e-books are available at AARP's online bookstore and through local and online bookstores.

**AARP.ORG/CAREGIVING (WWW.AARP.ORG/CAREGIVING):** Provides tools, information, and support available for family caregivers. Find an online community of other family caregivers, learn about local services, get helpful information, and connect with others who understand caregiving challenges.

**BOOKS ON FAMILY, CAREGIVING AND HOME (WWW.AARP.ORG/CAREGIVINGBOOKS):** Showcases books on home, family, and caregiving, including *Checklist for My Family*, a guide through the process of organizing your finances, legal documents, online accounts, wishes about medical care, and more.

**AARP.ORG/LIVABLE:** Offers articles and resources about home remodeling and housing options, as well as AARP's Livability Index (http://livabilityindex.aarp.org), where you can plug in zip codes to help decide where to live or to retire based on schools, housing costs, taxes, weather, local government, community activities, recreation, volunteer opportunities, and a host of other details.

**AARP HOMEFIT GUIDE (WWW.AARP.ORG/HOMEFIT):** Provides smart solutions for making your home comfortable, safe, and a great fit.

# Notes

*"We shape our dwellings,
and afterwards
our dwellings shape us."*

——WINSTON CHURCHILL